School Shootings In USA 2022

LAURA ANDERSON

All rights reserved. No part of this book may be reproduced, stored in a retrieval system, or transmitted in any form or by any means – electronic, mechanical, photocopying, recording, or otherwise – without the written permission of the Author copyright © 2022 Laura Anderson

TABLE OF CONTENTS

1
What happened?

2
Where did it work out?

3
Who was the shooter?

4
What are the public authority position on this?

5
What might have caused the shootings?

1
What happened?

- A teen shooter killed no less than 19 small kids and two grown-ups at Robb Elementary School - which shows in excess of 500 for the most part Hispanic and financially impeded understudies - in Texas on Tuesday.

- Every one of the 21 casualties were in a solitary 4th grade study hall.

- As per specialists, the shooting began at 11:32am (16:32 GMT).

- It was expressed that the shooter shot his grandma prior to going to the school where he deserted his vehicle and entered with a handgun and a rifle. Different authorities said later that the grandma made due and was being dealt with, however her condition was not known.

- The shooter blockaded himself inside the school and traded gunfire with officials as they entered the structure, a representative for the Department of Homeland Security was wounded.

- The shooter was killed.

- Various kids have been wounded, it stays indistinct the number of.

2
Where did it take place?

- The assault occurred in Uvalde - a little local area of around 16,000 occupants around

129km (80 miles) west of San Antonio and around 113km (70 miles) from the Mexican boundary.

3
Who was the gunman?

- The suspect as Salvador Ramos, an 18-year-old occupant of Uvalde and a US resident.
- Ramos worked at a café for a year however quit about a month prior.

- The specialists said he had lawfully bought two rifles and

375 rounds of ammo days before the shooting.

The shooter who killed 19 understudies and two educators at a Texas primary school Tuesday was in the vicinity for as long as an hour prior to policing entered a study hall and killed him.

4

What are the public authority position on this? Authorities all over the planet are answering the school shooting in Uvalde, Texas, the deadliest such occurrence to happen in the U.S. in almost 10 years.

In profound comments, an authority viewed it as a

Particularly American misfortune. He additionally expressed that we have emotional well-being issues, home grown questions in different nations, But these sorts of mass shootings never occur with the sort of recurrence that they occur in America.

5

What might have caused the shootings?

Lockdown Due to COVID-19

So the lockdown have decisively expanded examples of dysfunctional behavior among youngsters and in 10 days we have seen two mass shootings by unstable youngsters. Individuals are turning out to be deranged in light of the fact

that they are detached from others how might we associate them to other people and subsequently lessen the occasion of psychological sickness.

Emotional wellness Issues

Emotional wellness was a justification behind the shooting and excused the possibility that new weapon guidelines were required

One thing that has significantly changed is the situation with psychological wellness in our networks. We as a state, we as a general public, need to improve with emotional well-being. Anyone who shoots another person has an emotional well-being challenge.

A Lack of Guns in Schools

A few legislators have contended that mass shootings in schools could be better forestalled assuming that schools have more firearms in them, kept by either educators or security. Putting more equipped officials in schools or giving educators firearms would forestall mass shootings. Additionally positioning more

equipped cops at schools, would be more viable than fixing weapon control regulations.

The best apparatus for protecting children is

furnished policing the grounds.

Opened Doors at Schools

It was proposed that school formats expected to change to forestall mass shootings. He expressed that there ought to be one entryway for entry and exit from the school and no opened secondary passages.

The executioner entered here the same way the executioner entered at Sante Fe, through a secondary passage, an opened secondary passage.

Having one entryway that goes all through the school and having outfitted cops at that one entryway ought to be encouraged.

Kids Not Being Home Schooled

It was recommended that the taking shots at the grade school reinforced the contention for self-teaching.

The Impact of Social Media

The impact of web-based entertainment was applicable to the shooting.

The web-based entertainment applications, this dopamine dependence that they have given us all, our cell phones, they are our foes. They are separating our human association, Salvador Ramos carried on with an extremely confined life. This entire world we have fabricated, this virtual entertainment lattice, isn't really great for our psyches. Bring it down to these children, and how they constructed their whole lives around their web-based entertainment stages. 'How might I be renowned?' And they couldn't care less the way in which you become popular over virtual entertainment, assuming it's the butcher of other people or on the other hand on the off chance that it's shaking your backside in an exposed fashion on OnlyFans accounts. Anything that it takes.

Made in United States
Orlando, FL
11 November 2023